Money Past, Present, & Future:

From Financial Chaos to Financial Collaboration

Michael Martin

This book is dedicated to my love, my life, my wife Jesi

Without your unwavering support, this book would not have been possible

Personal finances tend to be a turbulent mix of what bills are due, when do I get paid, and how will I ever afford this emergency?! This book provides *initial guidance and thoughts* on how we see money, how we currently use money, and how we are, or aren't, preparing for our financial future. There are many personal finance books available, but none of them can provide a complete guide for each and every person. Personal finances are just that, personal! Please note many financial experts will tell you to just buy their book or course and you should be all set. This could not be further from the truth! The benefit of having a Personal Financial Coach to guide you during your Financial Fitness journey cannot be overstated. Money discussions can become emotional, as you uncover your own money past while reading this book and participating in coaching sessions. I want to make it clear that money behaviors do not affect your value as a human. Everyone sees money differently, and it is common to have uneasy feelings during your journey to Financial Fitness. I am not here to judge your financial condition, condemn your money behaviors, or devalue you as a human being. My job, as a Personal Financial Coach, is to provide insight and guidance as you complete your Financial Fitness journey. Every human is valuable and has their own special place in this world, regardless of how they choose to manage their finances. Helping others is a deep-rooted passion of mine and is the fundamental reason I started **BlueCollarBudgets.com**. I can take financial chaos and turn it into financial collaboration *with you* to achieve your desired level of Financial Fitness! The topics covered in this book are intimately connected to the topics we will discuss during your coaching sessions, but it is not an exhaustive list or meant to be used as a substitute for financial coaching sessions. My goal, for each person who reads this book and <u>schedules coaching sessions</u>, is to help you visualize your Financial Fitness journey and achieve your desired results!

Table of Contents

Section 1: Money Past

"Growth takes place when you seek grace and knowledge."

2 Peter 3:18

Feelings about Money

When you received your first official paycheck, what emotions went through your mind? Happiness? Joy? Honor? Relief? Anxiety? All these emotions and more are likely to have crossed your mind the day you were first paid. All the demanding work you put in finally paid off and now you can reap what was sown. I distinctly remember my first official paycheck like it was yesterday. Sure, I had been paid to do some small jobs and/or chores around the house, but this feeling was completely different. This money was mine in a distinct way!

Before we dive into learning how to manage our finances, we first need to unpack how each of us feel about money. Every person sees money differently. As a financial coach my job is to help you achieve Financial Fitness by understanding how you see money as an individual. For married couples, the complexity of financial discussions increases since there are two individuals involved who have differing money pasts. Understanding your Money Past is a critical part of the journey as it will affect what steps we can and cannot take in future coaching sessions. Answer the following questions on your own so that you can better understand how you feel about money:

1. Do you freely and openly discuss money topics with family (e.g., spouses, children)?

2. Do you constantly check your bank account balance online or through a mobile app?

3. Do you consider yourself a Spender or a Saver?

4. Are you concerned about running out of money every week and/or month?

5. If you won the lottery today, do you think any problems you are currently facing would disappear?

6. When you receive your paycheck, SSI, or disability income, do you have a plan for that money?

7. Do you use a credit card to pay for items you know you cannot currently afford?

8. Do you know your current overall financial condition (assets, liabilities, expenses, income, etc.)?

9. If a $500 emergency happened right now, do you have cash available to cover the emergency?

10. If married, do you keep purchases from your spouse? (e.g., hiding purchases in closet, paying with credit card, pretending item was a gift for someone else, etc.)

The above list of questions has, hopefully, allowed you to start thinking about how you see money, and the feelings you have surrounding personal finances in general. During your coaching sessions, we will go through these questions in order to get a clearer picture of your Money Past. Your answers will likely change as your money behaviors change, which is completely acceptable and expected. You will start to see how your Money Past has shaped your view of money up until this point in your life, and how we can change your mindset around money to better align with your goals individually and together as a couple, if applicable.

Parental Finances

It is likely most of your money behaviors are learned habits that you picked up from your parents, grandparents, or guardians. These behaviors were subconsciously learned over the course of many years and if needed, will take considerable effort on your part to re-define your new money behaviors. By first acknowledging your current perspective of money and how you interact with it, we can start to change the subconscious behaviors that are causing you financial stress during coaching sessions. As a reminder from the foreword, your money behaviors do not define who you are as a complete person. You are much more than how you manage your finances, and I need you to see how valuable you are as a human!

Adults today, with parents who are baby boomers, were told to save, save, save! While that is okay advice, it likely came from your parents being able to put money in a savings account or Certificate of Deposit (CD) that was paying 10-15% APY interest. This is currently not applicable to today's standard savings accounts or CDs that are barely paying 2-3% APY interest. Only recently, during periods of higher-than-expected inflation in 2021-23, has the option to use high-yield savings account (HYSA) or CDs been a part of personal finance discussions. While being told to save is still good advice, a better phrase to use would be "Always spend less than you _bring home_." Notice I said "…than you bring home" versus "your salary." This difference is important because if your first job pays you a salary of $55,000 per year this does not mean you are actually bringing home the entire $55,000! If you base any budget on salary alone, you will have a losing strategy from the beginning. During coaching sessions, we will focus only on your actual paycheck amounts (net income) and less on your salary/hourly wage (gross income). Your net income (paycheck) is likely 20-30% less than your gross income (salary or hourly wage). This large difference is due to payroll taxes, health insurance, child support, retirement, etc., and it is important to only focus on the amount you bring home for budgeting.

We understand that the financial orientation our parents, grandparents and guardians came from worked great during their formative years. However, we know future economic conditions will most certainly be different, therefore it is important for us to adapt in order to be successful with money moving forward.

Understanding Behavior & Change

The simple definition of behavior is the way something or someone acts on a regular and consistent basis. In this book, we want to focus on how you behave with your money. Do you have good or bad money behaviors? In this context, 'good' or "bad" refers to how well your current financial condition aligns with your longer-term money goals. In no way does good or bad money behavior dictate that you are a good or bad person (see Foreword). My guess is, however, since you are reading this book, you might be curious enough to see if your money behaviors are good or bad for your future Financial Fitness.

The simple definition of change is to make something or someone different; to alter or modify. Change is a straightforward concept in theory, but when we try to put it into practice it somehow overwhelms most of us. This is where having a personal financial coach on your side, helping you push through the financial pain can greatly improve your odds of success! For instance, we all know that everyone's New Year's resolution at some point in time has been to lose a few pounds. How many of us were successful on our own? How many are still going to the gym regularly in March? In August? How many of us, new to the gym, watched those with personal trainers achieve results while we floundered around and had no **_external_** accountability? Having a personal financial coach that cares about you and who is willing to guide you and push you, even when you do not think it is possible, can make all the difference!

During our coaching sessions, we will openly discuss money behaviors that are good as well as those that are bad and do not align with your financial goals. I have honest conversations with clients about how they choose to spend their money in a way that may be hurting their financial aspirations. If you have credit card debt, yet continually spend every weekend going out to bars buying shots for everyone, on the credit card that is nearly maxed out, I will ask you if you are serious about your Financial Fitness. I will provide insight into how you can make little but consistent changes to your behaviors so that we alter them to better suit your financial needs. My goal is not to have you beat yourself up over "bad" money behaviors. However, it is my job (and this is why you hired me) to help you see behaviors that can have adverse effects on the goals you have stated you want to achieve.

Admittance of Money Behaviors

Now we are getting to the good introspective parts! Since you've answered some preliminary money questions, what have you learned about how you see money? Are you a spender or a saver? Do you use money to escape reality? These questions help to emphasize how we see ourselves and how we perceive money. Also, these questions allow you to see how your current perception of money could be causing various financial difficulties within your life. Again, I am compelled to mention that your money behaviors do not determine your worth as a human. You are special and worthy, and my wish is that you realize there is hope for you if you are in a desperate financial position. The answers to these questions can reveal that there is another way, another path that can be taken that leads to your best version of Financial Fitness! If you know your current money behaviors and want to change them, continue reading and schedule a consultation so we can get started right away!

Section 2: Money Present

"So be careful to live your life wisely, not foolishly"

Ephesians 5:15

Budget Basics

When most people hear the term "budget" they instantly create images of restrictive spending, someone they might classify as "poor" or living paycheck-to-paycheck, and that is not how they want to be perceived by others. First, let me dispel all those rumors as categorically false! Social media has us brainwashed to believe that everyone is wealthy, and if you are not rich then there is something wrong with you. This is also incorrect and can lead to self-destruction. As a full-time personal financial coach, it is hard to see clients suffering under this perceived societal pressure. A budget, in its simplest form, is a document that gives you the ability to decide how your income is spent, as well as keeping track of progress on short and long-term goals. Creating a budget allows you the ability to control your finances rather than your finances controlling you! However, before we create our first budget, we must take a critical first step that separates **BlueCollarBudgets.com** from other financial coaches, gurus, or experts.

Tracking Expenses

Every financial guru or expert I have come across states the first step to do is to make a budget. How are you supposed to make a budget if you have no idea where every dollar of your income goes? If you follow these instructions your budget will be incorrect, you will become discouraged, and will likely stop budgeting. You should know your big expenses (e.g., rent/mortgage, auto loan, utilities) but the rest of your expenses might be a mystery to you. For the first month, simply write down every time you spend money in a spiral notebook or journal. It is that simple! Every bill that gets paid, drive-thru meal, shopping trip, grocery store trip, copay, etc. Just get in the habit of writing down *every single expense* for the first month using pen and paper (See Appendix 1). This action helps to create a more intimate connection with your finances than using an app on your phone or just looking at your credit/debit card statement. The goal of this first stage is to help you understand the difference between your regular monthly bills (e.g., rent/mortgage, utilities, auto loan, student loan, etc.) and the amount you **actually** spend each month!

Analyzing Expenses

Most people are completely surprised at the end of the first month of tracking their expenses when they finally understand why they feel like they are underperforming financially!

They can see that, on average, individuals/families spend just as much, if not more, on their variable monthly expenses (dining out, shopping, fuel, groceries, etc.) as they do on their fixed monthly expenses (rent/mortgage, utilities, auto loan, student loan, etc.). Often it is at this point, clients understand they might have a **spending problem**, not necessarily an *income problem*. Once this realization occurs for my clients, we can spend time figuring out how/why we spend money the way we do, and how those actions are having a real-time impact on your financial success. While we analyze expenses, we will also discuss good debt vs bad debt from a personal finance perspective, as well as strategies for eliminating the bad debt. There are two main perspectives for managing bad debt payments: Debt Snowball or Debt Avalanche. Depending on how you view money, we will select a method and develop a financial plan to get you out of bad debt as quickly as possible. This is one of the more critical steps in your Financial Fitness journey and will likely be difficult. I will coach you through the process, provide guidance, and listen to your feelings and concerns.

Connect with Your Money!

After you have a month of tracking expenses under your belt, then we start to create your first monthly budget. In this budget, we will need to account for a few annual/semi-annual expenses (e.g., car insurance, renter's insurance), variable salaries (if applicable), and overall credit card debt. You will bring this information to your coaching session so that we can see how to structure your monthly budget. When we structure your budget, the decisions about what to reduce or increase will be your choice with guidance from me (see Figure 1). A topic that will be covered in more detail during coaching sessions is your Expense-to-Income Ratio. In simple terms, it is a way to quickly see how much of your income you are spending regularly on expenses. Most clients start out with an expense-to-income ratio greater than one, meaning their expenses are higher than their income! One aspect of your budget that must be firm is the way to start saving money in an emergency fund. At Blue Collar Budgets, I start clients off by working to save $500 in an emergency fund that is strictly used for emergencies, not to cover other parts of budget shortfalls. $500 might seem low but I choose that amount for two particularly important reasons. One, $500 will generally cover a brief, non-severe emergency to keep you from using your credit card. Two, it provides a quick milestone that you can achieve and start to see progress. If you can save $500 in an emergency fund within 1-2 months, you start to believe that changing your behaviors will have a positive impact on your daily life. For those that might be in financial trouble or who feel like they have dug a hole they cannot get out of, there is help at **BlueCollarBudgets.com**!

Figure 1. Sample Budget

Sample Budget Spreadsheet

Fixed Expenses		Variable Costs	
Rent/Mortgage		Fuel	
Utilities		Dining Out	
Internet		Groceries	
Cell Phone Bill		Food Subtotal	$ -
Car Insurance		Shopping	
Credit Card debt		Entertainment	
Auto Loan Debt		Charity/Donations	
Student Loan Debt		Health/Wellness	
Subscriptions		Technology	
		Family Birthdays/Events	
Fixed Subtotal	$ -	Car 1 Taxes/Maintenance	
		Car 2 Taxes/Maintenance	
		Medical/Co-pays	
Income		Medications	
Paycheck Amount 1		Misc.	
Paycheck Amount 2			
Paycheck Amount 3			
Paycheck Amount 4		Variable Subtotal	$ -
Total Income	$ -	A	
Total Monthly Expenses (Fixed + Var)	$ -	B	

If Box B is larger than Box A, you spend more than you make each month!

Schedule a Free 15 minute consultation with BlueCollarBudgets.com!

Implement Plan

While discussing and finalizing your first monthly budget, you will also write down some short-term financial goals that can be completed in 3-6 months. Depending on your current level of Financial Fitness, the budget developed during coaching sessions will be more or less restrictive in order to achieve your short-term goals. However, remember that you already have one month of tracking expenses completed and have achieved a milestone on your Financial Fitness journey! Crafting a budget that allows you to live life as well as achieve your financial goals will take a few months of adjusting and correcting. As unforgiving debts (credit cards, auto loans, student loans, etc.) are paid down it will free up monthly income to be put towards other items in your budget. My commitment to you is simple, once your money goals have been confirmed, I will do everything in my power to help you realize those goals as quickly as possible. Some goals can be accomplished quickly, while others require additional time and effort to achieve. Regardless of how long it takes, I will be by your side guiding you on your journey to Financial Fitness.

Budget Breakthrough

At this point, you have mastered two out of five core competencies taught at Blue Collar Budgets (Budget Basics and Analyze/Implement Plan)! This is a wonderful achievement, and you have seen your Financial Fitness level surpass what you initially thought was possible. I call this stage Budget Breakthrough because clients can now see how budgeting helps them determine where their money goes. During this stage, you will also want to expand your emergency savings by another $500 ($1,000 total). This increase is made to cover some deductibles for more severe emergencies. It is also done at the beginning of this stage to ensure we have a proper foundation in place before moving on to the next steps. The Budget Breakthrough stage also allows clients to look back on all their progress, all the debt they have paid off, the sacrifices made, and the goals achieved. It is at this time that the coaching sessions turn from short-term thinking to more long-term focused. What are your goals in 5 years? 10 years? 30 years? Do you want to start a family or pay for your kids' college education? Do you want to spend retirement traveling the world? Do you want to open a business one day? We get to discuss all the possibilities that are in front of you now that you have conquered the difficult first steps of tracking expenses, building and keeping a budget, paying off crushing debt, and achieving huge milestones in your Financial Fitness journey! After defining your new monthly budget and long-term goals, you will further expand your emergency fund to cover three months' worth of expenses. This additional increase in emergency funds may seem trivial.

However, three months' worth of expenses in an emergency fund should help to stabilize your finances for a short time during job loss, medical leave, or any other longer lasting emergency. Keep reading to see what is in store for your Money Future now that you have turned behaviors into beliefs!

Section 3: Money Future

Peace

What does it feel like to have "bad" debt paid off? A huge weight off your shoulders is an understatement for most people. No more sleepless nights wondering how your bills will get paid. You no longer have the feeling you are financially drowning and cannot see the shore. You have conquered your Money Past, mastered your Money Present, and glanced toward your Money Future. Peace is such a simple word but when combined with your finances can have an enormous impact on your daily life. Peace that all your bills will be covered, and you will have money left over each month! Peace that you can focus on long-term goals like buying a house, investing, or increasing your gifts to charitable organizations. Peace that you have control over your finances rather than your finances controlling you!

Long-term goals should have a time horizon, the amount of time needed to achieve goal, of at least 3 to 30+ years. Deciding how to prioritize your long-term goals will be one of your last in-depth coaching sessions with me. You will want to write down your hopes and dreams. Envision how you want your life to look in the next several years and decades. Once you have some ideas, we can create a long-term financial goal roadmap to help you visualize progress as you continue your Financial Fitness journey. This is a tool you will use to keep yourself out of financial trouble in the future and remain financially stable through the future difficulties that may occur during our lives. It will also help to keep you from getting bored with budgeting and subsequently reverting back to your Money Past!

Purpose

Now that you have peace with your finances, and the financial journey has started a slower, more intentional pace, we must make sure complacency does not creep into our finances. Sometimes, clients see the huge relief of paying off debt and relaxing of monthly financial conditions as a path to incur more unmanageable debt again. Imagine starting with Blue Collar Budgets with no money left at the end of the month to now have several hundred or even several thousand dollars 'extra' each month. It is life-changing for sure, but it can also lead to future financial trouble if you do not stay vigilant. Companies spend billions of dollars each year on advertisements and marketing campaigns to get you to believe you absolutely must purchase their products. Do not let yourself become tempted by their tricks! They want *your* hard-earned money to make themselves wealthier. The first signs you are becoming financially bored is that you stop using a budget each month and stop tracking your expenses. These little steps give way to a very slippery slope that can easily lead to financial troubles again. This is the reason I take my time at the beginning of your coaching sessions to try and ensure you understand the process, why it works, and the common pitfalls along the way.

An easy way to ensure you remain on track to Financial Fitness is to keep staggered long-term goals. Having long-term goals at 3, 5, 7 years and so on helps to ensure you recognize almost instantly when you are deviating from your financial path. Correcting little missteps along the way is much easier and less time-consuming than waiting 7 years down the road and realizing you started veering off your financial path 6 years ago! Long-term goals have a way of adjusting our focus to a point in the future, like a beacon of light in a dark sea, which can help to guide you through the waves of life. Guidance is important because it is easy to forget future goals when the present is constantly begging for your attention. For example, losing your job, a car wreck, sickness, etc. can all have a huge impact on your finances and daily life. By keeping your perspective on a long-time horizon, it can be easier to manage your daily financial life.

Investing Basics

Once you have paid off your "bad" debt, have your monthly finances in order, and written down long-term goals, we can begin the discussion about investing. This section is not meant to cover all the investing basics, only those in relation to monthly budgeting. There are legal requirements that Blue Collar Budgets does not meet when providing investment advice and therefore this section is meant as strictly an overview of investing and not specific investment advice. Since you are now living well below your income level (total monthly expenses are no more than 85% of your NET income) each month, we can discuss the idea of investing. If we introduce investing too early in the process, before we have a firm financial foundation built, we risk it all collapsing down the road. Losing 1-2 years of investing on a 30-year time horizon is worth gaining the long-term financial knowledge and discipline to succeed with money. Often when investing is introduced without preparation, people will use their investment accounts as an emergency fund by pulling money out when needed. They also tend to experience anxiety when they see the stock market volatility and have a knee-jerk reaction, creating taxable events that can have a dramatic impact on their personal finances come tax season!

Most people consider investing to mean buying stocks of companies and holding them over a long enough period that they appreciate in value. However, you can also purchase corporate or government bonds (debt notes), Certificates of Deposit (CDs), Real Estate Investment Trusts (REITs), etc. and hopefully their value will increase over time, or they will pay you interest while they utilize your investment. Another simple option that investors may use is to purchase index funds, mutual funds, or exchange-traded funds (ETFs) either inside a workplace retirement plan (e.g., 401k), a brokerage account, or an individual retirement plan (e.g., IRA). There are plenty of options available when you reach this stage, and you should consult a registered investment advisor, certified financial planner, or certified financial advisor for individual financial investment advice. My goal is to ensure the *amount* you invest each month does not cause undue stress on your monthly budget and that all your "bad" debt has been eliminated. If this is the case, start out small with investing because it is tough to see balances lose value over a short time perspective. Stocks, bonds, and most all other investments have variability in their returns on a short timescale, and from a personal finance standpoint I want to ensure your foundation for long-term investments is firmly in place.

Expand Emergency Fund

Another reason not to put all your excess monthly income in the stock market is you also want to keep increasing your emergency fund to a minimum of 4-6 months' worth of living expenses (determined by your budget). If you are very conscious of your lifestyle and monthly spending habits, you can probably get away with only 3 months of expenses in a savings account that is strictly used for emergencies. This means if your monthly expenses total $4,000/month, you need a minimum of $12,000 sitting in a savings account that can be accessed quickly. However, if you feel comfortable with 5 months of expenses, that would be $20,000! These funds are not to be used for splurging on a vacation or buying something nice for your birthday. This money is to be out of sight, out of mind until an emergency happens, then and only then can these funds be utilized.

Generational Impact

We are nearly at our conclusion, and I want us to take a moment to look back at what has been accomplished over the course of many coaching sessions and quite possibly several years' worth of effort on your part. Starting out by acknowledging your Money Past, tracking your expenses, building and maintaining a monthly budget in your Money Present. Achieving peace of mind, giving your finances a purpose, and investing in your Money Future, you have certainly come a long way on your Financial Fitness journey. Lastly, we want to cover how this change of life you have experienced should not stop with you. You can push to make a generational impact with the skills you have learned and help those around you!

For those of you with children, hopefully during your Financial Fitness journey you have started to share good financial habits with your children. If not, I encourage you to start that conversation now. Look back at your first month of tracking expenses and then the most current month of expenses and compare the two. Let your children see how your Money Past is different than your Money Present, and how you are helping them with your Money Future. If old enough, let them manage the budget for a month, provided the necessities are covered.

Show them that in order to purchase an item they want, something else must be given up. This helps your children learn what true opportunity cost is and how to navigate that when they are older.

For those of you without children or spouses, you could start a local budget help group on Facebook or have a personal finance meeting with friends and family once a quarter. Starting more discussions about personal finances helps to remove the built-up stigma that currently surrounds money and openly discussing it. Many clients, at the beginning of coaching sessions, are scared or embarrassed to discuss their finances, but the more we openly discuss them with others the easier it becomes. Over time, we can erase the taboo surrounding personal finances so that everyone has access to the skills and knowledge necessary for their own Financial Fitness journey.

Increase Investing

As you continue to succeed with your finances, I encourage you to take any raise or bonus received from work and try to invest that money today, rather than allowing lifestyle creep. Investing today at the highest rate possible in your budget will allow more freedom and flexibility later in life. Most financial experts recommend trying to invest at least 20% of your income so you will have sufficient funds available for withdrawal during your retirement years. The longer you wait to pay off "bad" debt and start on your Financial Fitness journey the higher that percentage will need to be, which can feel impossible. However, my goal is to help you see that with the right coach, right tools, and right mindset it is not only possible, but attainable for anyone willing to put in the effort!

Conclusion

74% of Americans live paycheck-to-paycheck, and they will rely solely on a Social Security check to live on during retirement. The average American spends so much money on items they do not need, entire business models are built on having somewhere to store those unused items. Every time you purchase an item, you are exchanging the time it took to create the money to purchase that item. Time is a limited resource for everyone, and no amount of money can buy more of it. You only have one life to live, and it is up to you to decide how you spend your time and money. The average American has so much debt trying to "keep up with the Joneses", buying the newest cell phone, purchasing an ATV, buying a boat/RV, shopping excessively, etc. that their finances are on the brink of disaster!

If I can leave you with a few words of wisdom, let it be this: Make a financial plan and forge a new path for you, your family, and those around you. Do not settle for being average, you deserve a life and a legacy that is extraordinary!

Schedule a Consultation Today!

www.bluecollarbudgets.com

Use coupon code: MONEY2023 **for 50% off**

your first 1-hour coaching session

Date	Category	Amount ($)

Date	Category	Amount ($)